Summary of

The Art
of the Deal

by Donald Trump

Instaread

Please Note

This is key takeaways & analysis

Table of Contents

Overview

The Art of the Deal by Donald Trump offers business advice and strategy through the lens of Trump's business deals and development projects as head of the Trump Organization. There is no typical week or project in Trump's work. His days are filled with phone calls and impromptu meetings, but the variety of relationships and investments he details paint a picture of how Trump cuts deals and earns multiple millions.

Having begun learning the real estate business in Brooklyn and Queens under his father, Fred Trump, in the 1970s, Donald Trump set his sights on loftier projects in Manhattan. He began buying hotels and properties, renovating and rebuilding to create grand structures such as New York's Trump Tower (1983), as well as numerous other hotels and projects. As his reputation and credibility grew, he stretched his sights to Atlantic City, where he built Trump Plaza (1984), a casino-hotel complex. Trump's growing empire required management not only of contractors and his own employees, but also of business partners, rivals, politicians, and the ever-critical members of the media.

Through his various ventures, Trump details his mistakes and successes, sharing the thinking and strategic choices that have led him to become one of America's most renowned business magnates. He offers lessons for readers not only on investment and development, but also business relationships and psychology more broadly.

The Art of the Deal was first published in 1987. Subsequent editions appeared in 1989 and 2004.

Important People

Donald Trump is the author of *The Art of the Deal*. Trump is an American investor and real estate magnate, and is chairman and president of the Trump Organization and founder of Trump Entertainment Resorts. He is a media celebrity, the author of several business books, and a candidate for the 2016 Republican nomination for president of the United States.

Barron Hilton is a business magnate and socialite who took over the Hilton Hotels Corporation from his father, Conrad Hilton. He held the position of president and chief executive officer until his retirement.

Ace Greenberg was chairman of the Executive Committee of the Bear Stearns Companies, Inc., a New York-based global investment bank and securities trading and brokerage firm.

Ed Koch is a lawyer and politician, who has served as a U.S. congressman and as mayor of New York City.

Ada Louise Huxtable was an architecture critic for the *New York Times* and a winner of the Pulitzer Prize for Criticism.

Maryanne Trump is Donald Trump's older sister and a senior judge of the US Court of Appeals for the Third Circuit.

Tony Schwartz is a businessman and journalist. He co-authored the book with Trump.

Fred Trump was Donald Trump's father. Fred Trump was a successful real estate developer in Brooklyn and Queens, and an important business mentor for his son.

Robert Trump is Donald Trump's brother. Robert Trump worked in the Trump Organization, overseeing his brother's casinos.

Ivana Trump is a Czech-American athlete and model who became Donald Trump's first wife. She assisted Trump in the management of numerous Trump enterprises until their divorce in 1992.

Key Takeaways

1. Trump learned the business from his father, but he also wanted to make his own mark and be more than Fred Trump's son.

2. In all business dealings, but especially in New York, networking and building relationships are crucial to success.

3. Making a deal isn't just about selling the worthiness of the deal, but also about selling yourself.

4. When making a deal, it's smart to convince the seller that what they have isn't worth much.

5. Another strategy in making a deal is to put down the competition.

6. To project an image of luxury and class, maintain high levels of cleanliness and impeccable upkeep.

7. Relentless persistence is key to success in business.

8. Controversy sells. Even bad press can be good for business — and it's cheaper than marketing.

Thank you for purchasing this Instaread book

**Download the Instaread mobile app to get
unlimited text & audio summaries
of bestselling books.**

Visit Instaread.co
to learn more.

Analysis

Key Takeaway 1

Trump learned the business from his father, but he also wanted to make his own mark and be more than Fred Trump's son.

Analysis

Trump credits his father with showing him the ropes and teaching him important skills in leadership, hard work, and management. But he wasn't content merely to continue in his father's footsteps.

What shines through all the chapters and all the various projects Trump discusses is his incredible, overarching ambition. He could easily have continued along the lines of his father's modest development projects in Brooklyn and Queens, and would have made a good living doing so. But Trump is obsessed with always doing bigger, better, and more. This aspect of his character is what drove him to Manhattan instead. It's what drove him to buy hotels no one else would touch, to propose grandiose projects that the media criticized, and to always insist on the finest, most expensive, most luxurious materials and designs. Trump's ambition is evident in the mere appearance of his buildings—flashy, eye-catching, monstrously tall. In some ways his character is reminiscent of the conquerors and emperors of an earlier era. Trump is, indeed, a modern-day emperor of sorts, bent not only on outdoing others—including his own father—but also on constantly outdoing himself with each new project.

Key Takeaway 2

In all business dealings, but especially in New York, networking and building relationships are crucial to success.

Analysis

One of Trump's first moves after settling in Manhattan was to begin networking, building relationships with people who will later become business partners, advisors, and customers. Relationships are as integral to his success as strategy, and Trump places a high value on working with people of integrity.

Trump often passes judgment on the character of some figure — minor or major — who plays a role in his business dealings. He is attentive to the character of everyone from his assistant to reporters to politicians. He may respect a person for one reason, but have a bad feeling about him or her for another reason. Without saying so explicitly, he makes it clear that his success rises and falls on his ability to build relationships, meet other people's needs, create trust, and return favors. When Trump likes someone, he's effusive in his praise and dedicated in his efforts to prove his loyalty and friendship. But when he perceives someone as unfair or dishonest, the deal is off and the relationship falls through. He understands, on the one hand, that these relationships are instrumental: for instance, contributing money is necessary to stay on the good side of certain politicians. On the other hand, he seems to derive genuine value and pleasure from the people with whom he makes deals. Relationships are not just a means to an end for Trump; they are, for him, part of the "fun" of working in the business of real-estate development.

Key Takeaway 3

Making a deal isn't just about selling the worthiness of the deal, but also about selling yourself.

Analysis

Early in his career, when he still lacks experience and credentials, Trump sells his enthusiasm and energy. Later, he has experience to point to, but above all, it's his name and his reputation that help him close on good deals.

Trump understands the importance of personal brand and charisma. To some extent, the notion of "selling" himself has a superficial quality: Trump is obsessed with the appearance of things — the kinds of suits people wear, what clubs they belong to, where they own homes, who they know, and so forth. He tries to present himself to others in line with these values of appearance, for instance, by telling people he runs the Trump Organization even before it has become much of an organization at all. But his insistence on selling himself also speaks to deeper qualities—such as his excitement for and dedication to a project, as well as his commitment to completing it on time and under budget. Both when he's new to development and when he's become an established name, Trump sells his deals by making personal appeals and promises. He sells not only the idea he has for a property, but also the idea of why he alone is capable of leading the project and completing it properly.

Key Takeaway 4

When making a deal, it's smart to convince the seller that what they have isn't worth much.

Analysis

When Trump wants to buy a Manhattan property in a run-down neighborhood during an economic downturn, he convinces the seller that he's crazy to even think of buying the property. By undervaluing it, Trump is able to close the deal at the price he wants.

This is one of many psychological tricks Trump likes to play when he makes a deal. There is no doubt that undercutting a seller's confidence in the value of their property can often be an effective strategy. Indeed, as Trump tells it, this method works for him time and again. The success of this trick uncovers the extent to which baseless assertions, grand displays of confidence, and general showmanship affect the negotiating and deal-making process. Though finances, charts, graphs, and bank appraisals all play a role in how deals are cut, it's clear from Trump's portrayals that much of his success lies in his ability to make people believe his claims — whatever they are.

Of course, this method also raises some ethical questions about the way Trump influences sellers' decision-making. Does his tendency toward exaggeration and even misrepresentation make these deals in any sense unfair or dishonest? Trump doesn't seem to think so; at least, he never suggests that he has any moral qualms with manipulating people this way. As he tells it, this is all part of the game, and if sellers fall for his ploy, then they don't deserve to win anyway.

Key Takeaway 5

Another strategy in making a deal is to put down the competition.

Analysis

When Trump's property at West 34th Street competes with other properties to become the site of New York's new Convention Center, he makes his case by talking about how horrible the other sites are. The strategy pays off, and he wins the contract.

A less combative and aggressive strategy might be to rely simply on the strengths of one's own deal rather than emphasizing all the faults and weaknesses — real or imagined — of others. Trump does play up the strengths of his own proposals, but his strategy never stops there. He also has to go on attack. Trump's penchant for criticizing his competitors and their proposals is particularly interesting in light of his extreme sensitivity toward personal attacks and critiques of any kind. He loathes people who criticize him, but he stakes many of his negotiations and proposals on this strategy of criticizing others. This attack strategy is indicative of the brutal, dog-eat-dog nature of the business world in which Trump operates. There is little room for kind words or gestures here. Trump is out to win and winning means everyone who isn't in business with him or whose interests oppose his own must lose. This is part of the sense in which Trump figures as a kind of conqueror.

Key Takeaway 6

To project an image of luxury and class, maintain high levels of cleanliness and impeccable upkeep.

Analysis

Despite the cost, Trump insists that the brass rails in the Trump atrium be polished twice monthly. He also has his security ensure that the pavement in front of Trump Tower is free of peddlers. He is selling a "wonderland," as he himself puts it, clear of the debris and ugliness of poverty and dirt.

Trump's obsession with making sure anything unclean or unpleasant isn't associated with or even visible near his properties is part of the way in which he tries to create a fantasy world for guests and customers. He explicitly understands that the glitz and glam of his developments are all about fantasy, but he doesn't pause to consider the larger ramifications of this enterprise. Many critics, like Ada Huxtable, lamented what she called the "superglitz" of Trump Tower and the elitism it celebrated. [1] Trump expresses little concern for the plight of the peddlers and doesn't seem in any way bothered with the idea of chasing them away just so that the entrance to his building looks nicer. Though Trump contributes to charities, he does not discuss any interest in confronting poverty or alleviating New York's many socioeconomic struggles. He does not appear to be interested in using his immense power, wealth, and connections to help deal with these issues. Rather, he wants to be sure that they don't soil his brand.

Key Takeaway 7

Relentless persistence is key to success in business.

Analysis

Trump doesn't take "no" for an answer. Many of his deals come through after he has placed countless calls and made personal visits, reiterating his interests and proposals. His refusal to give up is part of what helps him succeed.

Despite Trump's many faults, distortions, and questionable claims, many people admire his sheer persistence in the face of repeated refusals. He is unabashed in his willingness, even as a young man with few accomplishments to his name, to call up high-level executives and developers, introduce himself, and propose a deal. This dogged determination continues later in his career as he closes deals in part by being the guy who just won't give up. It's a lesson that might be applied to any number of pursuits, industries, and goals: Aptitude, credibility, and power are often part of the equation in creating a successful outcome, but in a competitive world, they aren't necessarily enough on their own. Relentless persistence can be the thing that makes the difference between the person who wins the contract and the one who loses it.

Key Takeaway 8

Controversy sells. Even bad press can be good for business — and it's cheaper than marketing.

Analysis

Trump is frequently irked by critics who don't like his design proposals and tends to find his treatment by reporters unfair. But he also learns the value of media coverage, which is free and which brings attention to his brand even when it's negative.

This insight, while useful for business magnates and brands, calls into question the critical function of the press and the nature of media attention more broadly: If even criticism and controversy can help a brand succeed, is the press really serving its purpose? Why do consumers respond positively, rewarding brands that have been treated in a less than favorable light by reporters? If attention is a good in and of itself, regardless of the nature of that attention, then it seems business empires like Trump's are very difficult to hold accountable in the press. The more they're written about and the more controversy they create, the more notorious they become. The issue raises the question of whether the media actually does the public a disservice by dwelling excessively on Trump.

Author's Style

Trump's book is part memoir and part business strategy. It interweaves his business philosophy, strategy, and advice with his personal experiences building the Trump Organization. This lends the book a very conversational tone, full of Trump's opinions about various controversies, business dealings, partners, and critics. The book is divided into 14 chapters, beginning with "A Week in the Life," followed by chapters that focus on some of his major projects and deals. These discussions often become very detailed in terms of outlining proposal specifications, complex arrangements between partners, and larger economic considerations.

Nevertheless, Trump's voice remains distinctive throughout the book: Even when describing financial minutiae, he maintains a casual style, making the book compelling and approachable even for readers who aren't well versed in business dealings and real-estate development. Part of what makes the book so personally distinct is the way Trump insistently inserts his perceptions, likes, and dislikes of all the people he deals with — from contractors to New York mayors to his brother and his own wife. The book is a commentary not only on how he built the Trump Organization but also on Trump's beliefs about relationships, personalities, triumph, and failure.

Author's Perspective

Trump's motivation is twofold: He writes, on the one hand, to document his personal rise to success and the many business deals he has put together over the years. He is eager to explain to the public why he has done so well and which strategies and philosophies have led him to succeed — despite the many critics he has faced. He also writes to share his knowledge about making deals and building business relationships with other people interested in his expertise. He catalogues both his mistakes and his successes as lessons in understanding what works and what doesn't when it comes to vying for a contract, dealing with politicians, facing down the press, building a brand, and creating trust with business partners.

~~~~ END OF INSTAREAD ~~~~

Thank you for purchasing this Instaread book

**Download the Instaread mobile app to get
unlimited text & audio summaries
of bestselling books.**

Visit Instaread.co
to learn more.

References

1. Huxtable, Ada Louise. "Donald Trump's Tower." *The New York Times.* May 6, 1984. Accessed January 20, 2016. http://www.nytimes.com/1984/05/06/magazine/l-donald-trump-s-tower-170724.html

Lightning Source UK Ltd.
Milton Keynes UK
UKHW021109021219
354619UK00018B/3719/P